DIVE
LOG BOOK

IF FOUND, PLEASE RETURN TO:

NAME: ____

ADDRESS:

____

____

____

Dive Number: _________________
Date: _____________________
Location: _________________________
Ocean: ___________________________

TIME IN	TIME OUT

Bar/psi
START

Bar/psi
END

SI | PG | PG

☐ Computer Dive

Bottom Time

Depth

RNT _______
ABT _______
TBT _______

VISIBILITY
____

TEMP: Air _______ Surface _______ Bottom _______

GEAR USED

BCD: _________________
Wetsuit: _____________
Fins: ________________
Weights: _____________ kg/lbs
Cylinder: ____________ liters

DIVE SHOP STAMP

☐ Steel   ☐ Aluminum

☐ Fresh   ☐ Salt   ☐ Shore   ☐ Boat   ☐ Drift   ☐ Night   ☐ Training

DIVE COMMENTS

____
____
____
____
____
____

Bottom Time to Date: ___________

Time of this Dive: _____________

Cumulative Dive Time: __________

Verification Signature
____

☐ Instructor   ☐ Divemaster   ☐ Buddy

Certification No: __________

Dive Number: ______________________
Date: ______________________
Location: ______________________
Ocean: ______________________

TIME IN	TIME OUT

Bar/psi START	Bar/psi END

SI	PG		PG

☐ Computer Dive

Bottom Time

Depth

RNT ______
ABT ______
TBT ______

VISIBILITY
____

TEMP: Air ______ Surface ______ Bottom ______

DIVE SHOP STAMP

GEAR USED

BCD: ______________________
Wetsuit: ______________________
Fins: ______________________
Weights: ______________________ kg/lbs
Cylinder: ______________________ liters

☐ Steel   ☐ Aluminum

☐ Fresh   ☐ Salt   ☐ Shore   ☐ Boat   ☐ Drift   ☐ Night   ☐ Training

DIVE COMMENTS

____
____
____
____
____
____

Bottom Time to Date: ______________

Time of this Dive: ______________

Cumulative Dive Time: ______________

Verification Signature
____

☐ Instructor   ☐ Divemaster   ☐ Buddy

Certification No: ______________

Dive Number: _____________________

Date: _____________________

Location: _____________________

Ocean: _____________________

TIME IN	TIME OUT

Bar/psi START	Bar/psi END

RNT ________
ABT ________
TBT ________

VISIBILITY
____

TEMP: Air ______ Surface ______ Bottom ______

GEAR USED

BCD: _____________________

Wetsuit: _____________________

Fins: _____________________

Weights: _____________ kg/lbs

Cylinder: _____________ liters

DIVE SHOP STAMP

☐ Steel   ☐ Aluminum

☐ Fresh   ☐ Salt   ☐ Shore   ☐ Boat   ☐ Drift   ☐ Night   ☐ Training

DIVE COMMENTS

____

____

____

____

____

____

Bottom Time to Date: _____________

Time of this Dive: _____________

Cumulative Dive Time: _____________

Verification Signature

____

☐ Instructor   ☐ Divemaster   ☐ Buddy

Certification No: _____________

Dive Number: ___________________

Date: _____________________________

Location: __________________________

Ocean: _____________________________

TIME IN	TIME OUT

Bar/psi START	Bar/psi END

SI | PG | PG

☐ Computer Dive

Bottom Time

Depth

RNT _______
ABT _______
TBT _______

VISIBILITY

____

TEMP: Air _______ Surface _______ Bottom _______

GEAR USED

BCD: _________________

Wetsuit: _______________

Fins: _________________

Weights: _____________ kg/lbs

Cylinder: _____________ liters

DIVE SHOP STAMP

☐ Steel   ☐ Aluminum

☐ Fresh   ☐ Salt   ☐ Shore   ☐ Boat   ☐ Drift   ☐ Night   ☐ Training

DIVE COMMENTS

____

____

____

____

____

____

Bottom Time to Date: ___________

Time of this Dive: _____________

Cumulative Dive Time: ___________

Verification Signature

____

☐ Instructor   ☐ Divemaster   ☐ Buddy

Certification No: __________

Dive Number: _________________

Date: _____________________________

Location: ___________________________

Ocean: _____________________________

TIME IN	TIME OUT

Bar/psi START	Bar/psi END

SI	PG		PG

☐ Computer Dive

Bottom Time

Depth

RNT _________
ABT _________
TBT _________

VISIBILITY

____

TEMP: Air _________ Surface _________ Bottom _________

GEAR USED

BCD: _________________

Wetsuit: _______________

Fins: _________________

Weights: ______________ kg/lbs

Cylinder: ______________ liters

DIVE SHOP STAMP

☐ Steel ☐ Aluminum

☐ Fresh ☐ Salt ☐ Shore ☐ Boat ☐ Drift ☐ Night ☐ Training

DIVE COMMENTS

____

____

____

____

____

____

Bottom Time to Date: ___________

Time of this Dive: _____________

Cumulative Dive Time: ___________

Verification Signature

____

☐ Instructor ☐ Divemaster ☐ Buddy

Certification No: _________

Dive Number: ___________________

Date: _____________________________

Location: _________________________

Ocean: ___________________________

TIME IN	TIME OUT

Bar/psi START	Bar/psi END

SI	PG		PG

☐ Computer Dive

Bottom Time

Depth

RNT ________
ABT ________
TBT ________

VISIBILITY
____

TEMP: Air ______   Surface ______   Bottom ______

GEAR USED

BCD: ________________

Wetsuit: ____________

Fins: _______________

Weights: ____________ kg/lbs

Cylinder: ___________ liters

DIVE SHOP STAMP

☐ Steel   ☐ Aluminum

☐ Fresh   ☐ Salt   ☐ Shore   ☐ Boat   ☐ Drift   ☐ Night   ☐ Training

DIVE COMMENTS

____

____

____

____

____

____

Bottom Time to Date: ___________

Time of this Dive: _____________

Cumulative Dive Time: __________

Verification Signature

____

☐ Instructor   ☐ Divemaster   ☐ Buddy

Certification No: _________

Dive Number: ________________

Date: ________________________

Location: ____________________

Ocean: _______________________

TIME IN	TIME OUT

Bar/psi START	Bar/psi END

SI	PG	PG

☐ Computer Dive

Bottom Time

Depth

RNT ________
ABT ________
TBT ________

VISIBILITY

____

TEMP: Air ______ Surface ______ Bottom ______

GEAR USED

BCD: ________________

Wetsuit: ____________

Fins: ________________

Weights: ____________ kg/lbs

Cylinder: ____________ liters

DIVE SHOP STAMP

☐ Steel   ☐ Aluminum

☐ Fresh   ☐ Salt   ☐ Shore   ☐ Boat   ☐ Drift   ☐ Night   ☐ Training

DIVE COMMENTS

____

____

____

____

____

____

Bottom Time to Date: ____________

Time of this Dive: ______________

Cumulative Dive Time: ____________

Verification Signature

____

☐ Instructor   ☐ Divemaster   ☐ Buddy

Certification No: __________

Dive Number: _____________________

Date: _____________________

Location: _____________________

Ocean: _____________________

TIME IN	TIME OUT

Bar/psi START	Bar/psi END

SI	PG		PG

☐ Computer Dive

Bottom Time

Depth

RNT _______
ABT _______
TBT _______

VISIBILITY

____

TEMP: Air ______ Surface ______ Bottom _____

GEAR USED

BCD: _____________________

Wetsuit: _______________

Fins: _________________

Weights: _______________ kg/lbs

Cylinder: _____________ liters

DIVE SHOP STAMP

☐ Steel ☐ Aluminum

☐ Fresh ☐ Salt ☐ Shore ☐ Boat ☐ Drift ☐ Night ☐ Training

DIVE COMMENTS

____

____

____

____

____

____

Bottom Time to Date: ___________

Time of this Dive: _____________

Cumulative Dive Time: __________

Verification Signature

____

☐ Instructor ☐ Divemaster ☐ Buddy

Certification No: _________

Dive Number: ___________________
Date: _____________________
Location: _______________________
Ocean: _________________________

TIME IN	TIME OUT

Bar/psi START	Bar/psi END

SI	PG

☐ Computer Dive

Bottom Time

Depth

PG

RNT ________
ABT ________
TBT ________

VISIBILITY
____

TEMP: Air ______ Surface ______ Bottom _____

GEAR USED

BCD: _________________
Wetsuit: _____________
Fins: _______________
Weights: ____________ kg/lbs
Cylinder: ____________ liters

DIVE SHOP STAMP

☐ Steel   ☐ Aluminum

☐ Fresh   ☐ Salt   ☐ Shore   ☐ Boat   ☐ Drift   ☐ Night   ☐ Training

DIVE COMMENTS

____
____
____
____
____
____

Bottom Time to Date: ___________

Time of this Dive: _____________

Cumulative Dive Time: ___________

Verification Signature

____
☐ Instructor   ☐ Divemaster   ☐ Buddy

Certification No: _________

Dive Number: ______________________

Date: ______________________

Location: ______________________

Ocean: ______________________

TIME IN	TIME OUT

Bar/psi START	Bar/psi END

SI | PG | PG

☐ Computer Dive

Bottom Time

Depth

RNT ______
ABT ______
TBT ______

VISIBILITY
____

TEMP: Air ______ Surface ______ Bottom ______

GEAR USED

BCD: ______________________

Wetsuit: ______________________

Fins: ______________________

Weights: ______________ kg/lbs

Cylinder: ______________ liters

DIVE SHOP STAMP

☐ Steel ☐ Aluminum

☐ Fresh ☐ Salt ☐ Shore ☐ Boat ☐ Drift ☐ Night ☐ Training

DIVE COMMENTS

____
____
____
____
____
____

Bottom Time to Date: ______________

Time of this Dive: ______________

Cumulative Dive Time: ______________

Verification Signature
____

☐ Instructor ☐ Divemaster ☐ Buddy

Certification No: ______________

Dive Number: _______________________

Date: _______________________

Location: _______________________

Ocean: _______________________

TIME IN	TIME OUT

Bar/psi START	Bar/psi END

SI | PG | PG

☐ Computer Dive

Bottom Time

Depth

RNT _______
ABT _______
TBT _______

VISIBILITY
____

TEMP: Air _______ Surface _______ Bottom _______

GEAR USED

BCD: _______________

Wetsuit: _______________

Fins: _______________

Weights: _______________ kg/lbs

Cylinder: _______________ liters

DIVE SHOP STAMP

☐ Steel ☐ Aluminum

☐ Fresh ☐ Salt ☐ Shore ☐ Boat ☐ Drift ☐ Night ☐ Training

DIVE COMMENTS

____

____

____

____

____

____

Bottom Time to Date: _______________

Time of this Dive: _______________

Cumulative Dive Time: _______________

Verification Signature

____

☐ Instructor ☐ Divemaster ☐ Buddy

Certification No: _______________

Dive Number: ______________________

Date: ______________________

Location: ______________________

Ocean: ______________________

TIME IN	TIME OUT

Bar/psi START	Bar/psi END

SI	PG		PG

☐ Computer Dive

Bottom Time

Depth

RNT ________
ABT ________
TBT ________

VISIBILITY
____

TEMP: Air ________ Surface ________ Bottom ________

GEAR USED

BCD: ______________________

Wetsuit: ______________________

Fins: ______________________

Weights: ______________________ kg/lbs

Cylinder: ______________________ liters

DIVE SHOP STAMP

☐ Steel   ☐ Aluminum

☐ Fresh   ☐ Salt   ☐ Shore   ☐ Boat   ☐ Drift   ☐ Night   ☐ Training

DIVE COMMENTS

____

____

____

____

____

____

Bottom Time to Date: ______________

Time of this Dive: ______________

Cumulative Dive Time: ______________

Verification Signature

____

☐ Instructor   ☐ Divemaster   ☐ Buddy

Certification No: ______________

Dive Number: ___________________

Date: ___________________

Location: ___________________

Ocean: ___________________

TIME IN	TIME OUT

Bar/psi START	Bar/psi END

| SI | PG | | PG |

☐ Computer Dive

Bottom Time

Depth

RNT ________
ABT ________
TBT ________

VISIBILITY
____

TEMP: Air ______ Surface ______ Bottom ______

GEAR USED

BCD: ___________________
Wetsuit: ___________________
Fins: ___________________
Weights: ___________________ kg/lbs
Cylinder: ___________________ liters

DIVE SHOP STAMP

☐ Steel ☐ Aluminum

☐ Fresh ☐ Salt ☐ Shore ☐ Boat ☐ Drift ☐ Night ☐ Training

DIVE COMMENTS

____
____
____
____
____
____

Bottom Time to Date: ___________

Time of this Dive: ___________

Cumulative Dive Time: ___________

Verification Signature

____

☐ Instructor ☐ Divemaster ☐ Buddy

Certification No: ___________

Dive Number: ______________________

Date: ______________________

Location: ______________________

Ocean: ______________________

| SI | PG | | PG |

☐ Computer Dive

Bottom Time

Depth

| TIME IN | TIME OUT |

Bar/psi
START

Bar/psi
END

RNT ________
ABT ________
TBT ________

VISIBILITY
____

TEMP: Air ______ Surface ______ Bottom ______

GEAR USED

BCD: ______________

Wetsuit: ______________

Fins: ______________

Weights: ______________ kg/lbs

Cylinder: ______________ liters

DIVE SHOP STAMP

☐ Steel   ☐ Aluminum

☐ Fresh   ☐ Salt   ☐ Shore   ☐ Boat   ☐ Drift   ☐ Night   ☐ Training

DIVE COMMENTS

____

____

____

____

____

____

Bottom Time to Date: ____________

Time of this Dive: ______________

Cumulative Dive Time: ____________

Verification Signature

____

☐ Instructor   ☐ Divemaster   ☐ Buddy

Certification No: __________

Dive Number: ___________________

Date: ___________________

Location: ___________________

Ocean: ___________________

TIME IN	TIME OUT

Bar/psi START	Bar/psi END

SI	PG		PG

☐ Computer Dive

Bottom Time

Depth

RNT _______
ABT _______
TBT _______

VISIBILITY
____

TEMP: Air _______ Surface _______ Bottom _______

DIVE SHOP STAMP

GEAR USED

BCD: ___________________

Wetsuit: ___________________

Fins: ___________________

Weights: ___________________ kg/lbs

Cylinder: ___________________ liters

☐ Steel   ☐ Aluminum

☐ Fresh   ☐ Salt   ☐ Shore   ☐ Boat   ☐ Drift   ☐ Night   ☐ Training

DIVE COMMENTS

____

____

____

____

____

____

Bottom Time to Date: ___________

Time of this Dive: ______________

Cumulative Dive Time: ___________

Verification Signature

____

☐ Instructor   ☐ Divemaster   ☐ Buddy

Certification No: __________

Dive Number: _________________

Date: _____________________

Location: __________________

Ocean: ____________________

TIME IN	TIME OUT

Bar/psi START	Bar/psi END

SI	PG		PG

☐ Computer Dive

Bottom Time

Depth

RNT _______
ABT _______
TBT _______

VISIBILITY
____

TEMP: Air _______ Surface _______ Bottom _______

GEAR USED

BCD: _________________

Wetsuit: _____________

Fins: ________________

Weights: ____________ kg/lbs

Cylinder: ____________ liters

DIVE SHOP STAMP

☐ Steel   ☐ Aluminum

☐ Fresh   ☐ Salt   ☐ Shore   ☐ Boat   ☐ Drift   ☐ Night   ☐ Training

DIVE COMMENTS

____

____

____

____

____

____

Bottom Time to Date: ___________

Time of this Dive: _____________

Cumulative Dive Time: __________

Verification Signature

____

☐ Instructor   ☐ Divemaster   ☐ Buddy

Certification No: _________

Dive Number: ___________________

Date: ___________________________

Location: _______________________

Ocean: _________________________

TIME IN	TIME OUT

Bar/psi START	Bar/psi END

☐ Computer Dive

Bottom Time

Depth

SI | PG | PG

RNT ________
ABT ________
TBT ________

VISIBILITY
____

TEMP: Air ______ Surface ______ Bottom ______

GEAR USED

BCD: ___________________

Wetsuit: ______________

Fins: __________________

Weights: _____________ kg/lbs

Cylinder: _____________ liters

☐ Steel   ☐ Aluminum

☐ Fresh   ☐ Salt   ☐ Shore   ☐ Boat   ☐ Drift   ☐ Night   ☐ Training

DIVE SHOP STAMP

DIVE COMMENTS

____

____

____

____

____

Bottom Time to Date: ___________

Time of this Dive: _____________

Cumulative Dive Time: __________

Verification Signature

____

☐ Instructor   ☐ Divemaster   ☐ Buddy

Certification No: __________

Dive Number: _______________________
Date: ____________________________
Location: _________________________
Ocean: ___________________________

TIME IN	TIME OUT

Bar/psi START	Bar/psi END

SI	PG		PG

☐ Computer Dive

Bottom Time

Depth

RNT _______
ABT _______
TBT _______

VISIBILITY

____

TEMP: Air ______ Surface ______ Bottom ______

GEAR USED

BCD: _________________
Wetsuit: _____________
Fins: _______________
Weights: _____________ kg/lbs
Cylinder: _____________ liters

DIVE SHOP STAMP

☐ Steel   ☐ Aluminum

☐ Fresh   ☐ Salt   ☐ Shore   ☐ Boat   ☐ Drift   ☐ Night   ☐ Training

DIVE COMMENTS

____

____

____

____

____

Bottom Time to Date: ___________

Time of this Dive: _____________

Cumulative Dive Time: ___________

Verification Signature

____

☐ Instructor   ☐ Divemaster   ☐ Buddy

Certification No: _________

Dive Number: _______________________
Date: _______________________
Location: _______________________
Ocean: _______________________

TIME IN	TIME OUT

Bar/psi
START

Bar/psi
END

SI | PG | PG

☐ Computer Dive

Bottom Time

Depth

RNT _______
ABT _______
TBT _______

VISIBILITY
____

TEMP: Air _______ Surface _______ Bottom _______

GEAR USED

BCD: _______________
Wetsuit: _____________
Fins: _______________
Weights: _____________ kg/lbs
Cylinder: _____________ liters

DIVE SHOP STAMP

☐ Steel   ☐ Aluminum

☐ Fresh   ☐ Salt   ☐ Shore   ☐ Boat   ☐ Drift   ☐ Night   ☐ Training

DIVE COMMENTS

____
____
____
____
____
____

Bottom Time to Date: _____________

Time of this Dive: _______________

Cumulative Dive Time: ___________

Verification Signature

____

☐ Instructor   ☐ Divemaster   ☐ Buddy

Certification No: __________

Dive Number: _______________________

Date: _______________________________

Location: ___________________________

Ocean: _____________________________

TIME IN	TIME OUT

Bar/psi START	Bar/psi END

| SI | PG | | PG |

☐ Computer Dive

Bottom Time

Depth

RNT _______
ABT _______
TBT _______

VISIBILITY

____

TEMP: Air _______ Surface _______ Bottom _______

GEAR USED

BCD: _________________

Wetsuit: _____________

Fins: ________________

Weights: _____________ kg/lbs

Cylinder: _____________ liters

DIVE SHOP STAMP

☐ Steel   ☐ Aluminum

☐ Fresh   ☐ Salt   ☐ Shore   ☐ Boat   ☐ Drift   ☐ Night   ☐ Training

DIVE COMMENTS

____

____

____

____

____

____

Bottom Time to Date: ___________

Time of this Dive: _______________

Cumulative Dive Time: ___________

Verification Signature

____

☐ Instructor   ☐ Divemaster   ☐ Buddy

Certification No: _________

Dive Number: _____________________

Date: ___________________________

Location: _______________________

Ocean: _________________________

TIME IN	TIME OUT

Bar/psi START	Bar/psi END

SI	PG		PG

☐ Computer Dive

Bottom Time

Depth

RNT ________
ABT ________
TBT ________

VISIBILITY
____

TEMP: Air ______ Surface ______ Bottom ______

GEAR USED

BCD: _________________

Wetsuit: ____________

Fins: _______________

Weights: ____________ kg/lbs

Cylinder: ____________ liters

DIVE SHOP STAMP

☐ Steel ☐ Aluminum

☐ Fresh ☐ Salt ☐ Shore ☐ Boat ☐ Drift ☐ Night ☐ Training

DIVE COMMENTS

____

____

____

____

____

____

Bottom Time to Date: ___________

Time of this Dive: ______________

Cumulative Dive Time: ___________

Verification Signature

____

☐ Instructor   ☐ Divemaster   ☐ Buddy

Certification No: _________

Dive Number: _____________________
Date: _____________________
Location: _____________________
Ocean: _____________________

TIME IN	TIME OUT

Bar/psi START	Bar/psi END

SI	PG		PG

☐ Computer Dive

Bottom Time

Depth

RNT _______
ABT _______
TBT _______

VISIBILITY
____

TEMP: Air _______ Surface _______ Bottom _______

GEAR USED

BCD: _____________________
Wetsuit: _______________
Fins: _______________
Weights: _______________ kg/lbs
Cylinder: _______________ liters

DIVE SHOP STAMP

☐ Steel ☐ Aluminum

☐ Fresh ☐ Salt ☐ Shore ☐ Boat ☐ Drift ☐ Night ☐ Training

DIVE COMMENTS

____
____
____
____
____
____

Bottom Time to Date: _____________

Time of this Dive: _______________

Cumulative Dive Time: _____________

Verification Signature

____

☐ Instructor ☐ Divemaster ☐ Buddy

Certification No: _____________

Dive Number: _______________________

Date: _______________________

Location: _______________________

Ocean: _______________________

TIME IN	TIME OUT

Bar/psi START	Bar/psi END

☐ Computer Dive

SI | PG

PG

Bottom Time

Depth

RNT _______
ABT _______
TBT _______

VISIBILITY
____

TEMP: Air _______ Surface _______ Bottom _______

GEAR USED

BCD: _______________

Wetsuit: _______________

Fins: _______________

Weights: _______________ kg/lbs

Cylinder: _______________ liters

DIVE SHOP STAMP

☐ Steel   ☐ Aluminum

☐ Fresh   ☐ Salt   ☐ Shore   ☐ Boat   ☐ Drift   ☐ Night   ☐ Training

DIVE COMMENTS

____

____

____

____

____

____

Bottom Time to Date: _______________

Time of this Dive: _______________

Cumulative Dive Time: _______________

Verification Signature

____

☐ Instructor   ☐ Divemaster   ☐ Buddy

Certification No: _______________

Dive Number: _______________________

Date: _________________________________

Location: _____________________________

Ocean: ________________________________

TIME IN	TIME OUT

Bar/psi START	Bar/psi END

SI	PG		PG

☐ Computer Dive

Bottom Time

Depth

RNT ________
ABT ________
TBT ________

VISIBILITY
____

TEMP: Air ______ Surface ______ Bottom ______

GEAR USED

BCD: _____________________

Wetsuit: _______________

Fins: _________________

Weights: ______________ kg/lbs

Cylinder: ______________ liters

DIVE SHOP STAMP

☐ Steel   ☐ Aluminum

☐ Fresh   ☐ Salt   ☐ Shore   ☐ Boat   ☐ Drift   ☐ Night   ☐ Training

DIVE COMMENTS

____

____

____

____

____

____

Bottom Time to Date: ______________

Time of this Dive: ________________

Cumulative Dive Time: ____________

Verification Signature

____

☐ Instructor   ☐ Divemaster   ☐ Buddy

Certification No: ____________

Dive Number: _________________

Date: _____________________________

Location: ___________________________

Ocean: ____________________________

TIME IN	TIME OUT

Bar/psi
START

Bar/psi
END

| SI | PG | | PG |

☐ Computer
Dive

Bottom Time

Depth

RNT _______
ABT _______
TBT _______

VISIBILITY

____

TEMP: Air _______ Surface _______ Bottom _______

GEAR USED

BCD: _________________

Wetsuit: _____________

Fins: _______________

Weights: _____________ kg/lbs

Cylinder: _____________ liters

DIVE SHOP STAMP

☐ Steel   ☐ Aluminum

☐ Fresh   ☐ Salt   ☐ Shore   ☐ Boat   ☐ Drift   ☐ Night   ☐ Training

DIVE COMMENTS

____

____

____

____

____

Bottom Time to Date: ___________

Time of this Dive: _____________

Cumulative Dive Time: ___________

Verification Signature

____

☐ Instructor   ☐ Divemaster   ☐ Buddy

Certification No: __________

Dive Number: ___________________
Date: ___________________
Location: ___________________
Ocean: ___________________

TIME IN	TIME OUT

Bar/psi START	Bar/psi END

☐ Computer Dive

SI | PG | PG

Bottom Time

Depth

RNT ________
ABT ________
TBT ________

VISIBILITY
____

TEMP: Air ______ Surface ______ Bottom ______

GEAR USED

BCD: ___________________
Wetsuit: ___________________
Fins: ___________________
Weights: ___________________ kg/lbs
Cylinder: ___________________ liters

DIVE SHOP STAMP

☐ Steel   ☐ Aluminum

☐ Fresh   ☐ Salt   ☐ Shore   ☐ Boat   ☐ Drift   ☐ Night   ☐ Training

DIVE COMMENTS

____
____
____
____
____
____

Bottom Time to Date: ___________

Time of this Dive: ___________

Cumulative Dive Time: ___________

Verification Signature

____

☐ Instructor   ☐ Divemaster   ☐ Buddy

Certification No: ___________

Dive Number: _____________________

Date: ____________________________

Location: ________________________

Ocean: ___________________________

TIME IN	TIME OUT

Bar/psi START	Bar/psi END

SI	PG		PG

☐ Computer Dive

Bottom Time

Depth

RNT _______
ABT _______
TBT _______

VISIBILITY
____

TEMP: Air _______ Surface _______ Bottom _______

GEAR USED

BCD: ___________________

Wetsuit: _____________

Fins: ________________

Weights: _____________ kg/lbs

Cylinder: _____________ liters

DIVE SHOP STAMP

☐ Steel ☐ Aluminum

☐ Fresh ☐ Salt ☐ Shore ☐ Boat ☐ Drift ☐ Night ☐ Training

DIVE COMMENTS

____

____

____

____

____

____

Bottom Time to Date: ____________

Time of this Dive: ______________

Cumulative Dive Time: ____________

Verification Signature

____

☐ Instructor ☐ Divemaster ☐ Buddy

Certification No: _________

Dive Number: _______________________

Date: _______________________

Location: _______________________

Ocean: _______________________

TIME IN	TIME OUT

Bar/psi START	Bar/psi END

| SI | PG | | PG |

☐ Computer Dive

Bottom Time

Depth

RNT _______
ABT _______
TBT _______

VISIBILITY

____

TEMP: Air _______ Surface _______ Bottom _______

GEAR USED

BCD: _______________________

Wetsuit: _______________________

Fins: _______________________

Weights: _______________ kg/lbs

Cylinder: _______________ liters

DIVE SHOP STAMP

☐ Steel   ☐ Aluminum

☐ Fresh   ☐ Salt   ☐ Shore   ☐ Boat   ☐ Drift   ☐ Night   ☐ Training

DIVE COMMENTS

____

____

____

____

____

____

Bottom Time to Date: _______________

Time of this Dive: _______________

Cumulative Dive Time: _______________

Verification Signature

____

☐ Instructor   ☐ Divemaster   ☐ Buddy

Certification No: _______________

Dive Number: _______________________

Date: _____________________________

Location: _________________________

Ocean: ____________________________

TIME IN	TIME OUT

Bar/psi START	Bar/psi END

SI	PG		PG

☐ Computer Dive

Bottom Time

Depth

RNT _______
ABT _______
TBT _______

VISIBILITY
____

TEMP: Air _______ Surface _______ Bottom _______

GEAR USED

BCD: _________________

Wetsuit: _____________

Fins: ________________

Weights: _____________ kg/lbs

Cylinder: ____________ liters

DIVE SHOP STAMP

☐ Steel   ☐ Aluminum

☐ Fresh   ☐ Salt   ☐ Shore   ☐ Boat   ☐ Drift   ☐ Night   ☐ Training

DIVE COMMENTS

____

____

____

____

____

____

Bottom Time to Date: ___________

Time of this Dive: _____________

Cumulative Dive Time: ___________

Verification Signature

____

☐ Instructor   ☐ Divemaster   ☐ Buddy

Certification No: _________

Dive Number: _______________
Date: _________________
Location: _______________
Ocean: __________________

TIME IN	TIME OUT

Bar/psi START	Bar/psi END

SI	PG		PG

☐ Computer Dive

Bottom Time

Depth

RNT _______
ABT _______
TBT _______

VISIBILITY

____

TEMP: Air _______ Surface _______ Bottom _______

GEAR USED

BCD: _________________
Wetsuit: _____________
Fins: ________________
Weights: ______________ kg/lbs
Cylinder: ____________ liters

DIVE SHOP STAMP

☐ Steel   ☐ Aluminum

☐ Fresh   ☐ Salt   ☐ Shore   ☐ Boat   ☐ Drift   ☐ Night   ☐ Training

DIVE COMMENTS

____

____

____

____

____

____

Bottom Time to Date: ___________

Time of this Dive: ______________

Cumulative Dive Time: __________

Verification Signature

____

☐ Instructor   ☐ Divemaster   ☐ Buddy

Certification No: _________

Dive Number: _____________________

Date: _____________________

Location: _____________________

Ocean: _____________________

TIME IN	TIME OUT

Bar/psi START	Bar/psi END

| SI | PG | | PG |

☐ Computer Dive

Bottom Time

Depth

RNT _______
ABT _______
TBT _______

VISIBILITY
____

TEMP: Air _______ Surface _______ Bottom _______

GEAR USED

BCD: _____________________
Wetsuit: _____________________
Fins: _____________________
Weights: _____________________ kg/lbs
Cylinder: _____________________ liters

DIVE SHOP STAMP

☐ Steel   ☐ Aluminum

☐ Fresh   ☐ Salt   ☐ Shore   ☐ Boat   ☐ Drift   ☐ Night   ☐ Training

DIVE COMMENTS

____

____

____

____

____

____

Bottom Time to Date: _____________

Time of this Dive: _____________

Cumulative Dive Time: _____________

Verification Signature

____

☐ Instructor   ☐ Divemaster   ☐ Buddy

Certification No: _____________

Dive Number: ___________________
Date: _______________________
Location: __________________________
Ocean: ____________________________

TIME IN	TIME OUT

| | SI | PG | | PG |

☐ Computer Dive

Bottom Time

Depth

| Bar/psi START | Bar/psi END |

RNT _______
ABT _______
TBT _______

VISIBILITY
____

TEMP: Air _______ Surface _______ Bottom _______

GEAR USED

BCD: ________________
Wetsuit: _____________
Fins: ________________
Weights: ____________ kg/lbs
Cylinder: ____________ liters

DIVE SHOP STAMP

☐ Steel ☐ Aluminum

☐ Fresh ☐ Salt ☐ Shore ☐ Boat ☐ Drift ☐ Night ☐ Training

DIVE COMMENTS

____

____

____

____

____

____

Bottom Time to Date: ___________

Time of this Dive: _____________

Cumulative Dive Time: __________

Verification Signature

____

☐ Instructor ☐ Divemaster ☐ Buddy

Certification No: ___________

Dive Number: _______________

Date: _______________

Location: _______________

Ocean: _______________

TIME IN	TIME OUT

Bar/psi START	Bar/psi END

SI	PG		PG

☐ Computer Dive

Bottom Time

Depth

RNT _______
ABT _______
TBT _______

VISIBILITY
____

TEMP: Air _______ Surface _______ Bottom _______

GEAR USED

BCD: _______________

Wetsuit: _______________

Fins: _______________

Weights: _______________ kg/lbs

Cylinder: _______________ liters

DIVE SHOP STAMP

☐ Steel   ☐ Aluminum

☐ Fresh   ☐ Salt   ☐ Shore   ☐ Boat   ☐ Drift   ☐ Night   ☐ Training

DIVE COMMENTS

____

____

____

____

____

____

Bottom Time to Date: _______________

Time of this Dive: _______________

Cumulative Dive Time: _______________

Verification Signature

____

☐ Instructor   ☐ Divemaster   ☐ Buddy

Certification No: _______________

Dive Number: ______________________

Date: ______________________

Location: ______________________

Ocean: ______________________

TIME IN	TIME OUT

Bar/psi START	Bar/psi END

SI	PG		PG

☐ Computer Dive

Bottom Time

Depth

RNT ________
ABT ________
TBT ________

VISIBILITY
____

TEMP: Air ______ Surface ______ Bottom ______

GEAR USED

BCD: ____________________

Wetsuit: ________________

Fins: __________________

Weights: ______________ kg/lbs

Cylinder: ______________ liters

DIVE SHOP STAMP

☐ Steel ☐ Aluminum

☐ Fresh ☐ Salt ☐ Shore ☐ Boat ☐ Drift ☐ Night ☐ Training

DIVE COMMENTS

____

____

____

____

____

____

Bottom Time to Date: ____________

Time of this Dive: ______________

Cumulative Dive Time: ____________

Verification Signature

____

☐ Instructor ☐ Divemaster ☐ Buddy

Certification No: ______________

Dive Number: _______________________

Date: _______________________

Location: _______________________

Ocean: _______________________

TIME IN	TIME OUT

Bar/psi START	Bar/psi END

| SI | PG | | PG |

☐ Computer Dive

Bottom Time

Depth

RNT _______
ABT _______
TBT _______

VISIBILITY
____

TEMP: Air _______ Surface _______ Bottom _______

GEAR USED

BCD: _______________

Wetsuit: _______________

Fins: _______________

Weights: _______________ kg/lbs

Cylinder: _______________ liters

DIVE SHOP STAMP

☐ Steel   ☐ Aluminum

☐ Fresh   ☐ Salt   ☐ Shore   ☐ Boat   ☐ Drift   ☐ Night   ☐ Training

DIVE COMMENTS

____

____

____

____

____

____

Bottom Time to Date: _______________

Time of this Dive: _______________

Cumulative Dive Time: _______________

Verification Signature

____

☐ Instructor   ☐ Divemaster   ☐ Buddy

Certification No: _______________

Dive Number: _________________

Date: _____________________

Location: _________________

Ocean: ___________________

SI	PG		PG

☐ Computer Dive

Bottom Time

Depth

TIME IN	**TIME OUT**

Bar/psi
START

Bar/psi
END

RNT _______
ABT _______
TBT _______

VISIBILITY
____

TEMP: Air _______ Surface _______ Bottom _______

GEAR USED

BCD: _________________

Wetsuit: _____________

Fins: _______________

Weights: ___________ kg/lbs

Cylinder: ___________ liters

DIVE SHOP STAMP

☐ Steel   ☐ Aluminum

☐ Fresh   ☐ Salt   ☐ Shore   ☐ Boat   ☐ Drift   ☐ Night   ☐ Training

DIVE COMMENTS

____

____

____

____

____

Bottom Time to Date: ___________

Time of this Dive: _____________

Cumulative Dive Time: ___________

Verification Signature

____

☐ Instructor   ☐ Divemaster   ☐ Buddy

Certification No: ___________

Dive Number: _______________

Date: _______________

Location: _______________

Ocean: _______________

TIME IN	TIME OUT

Bar/psi START	Bar/psi END

SI	PG		PG

☐ Computer Dive

Bottom Time

Depth

RNT ________
ABT ________
TBT ________

VISIBILITY
____

TEMP: Air ______ Surface ______ Bottom ______

DIVE SHOP STAMP

GEAR USED

BCD: _______________
Wetsuit: _______________
Fins: _______________
Weights: _______________ kg/lbs
Cylinder: _______________ liters

☐ Steel   ☐ Aluminum

☐ Fresh   ☐ Salt   ☐ Shore   ☐ Boat   ☐ Drift   ☐ Night   ☐ Training

DIVE COMMENTS

____

____

____

____

____

____

Bottom Time to Date: _______________

Time of this Dive: _______________

Cumulative Dive Time: _______________

Verification Signature

____

☐ Instructor   ☐ Divemaster   ☐ Buddy

Certification No: _______________

Dive Number: ___________________

Date: _____________________

Location: ___________________

Ocean: ______________________

TIME IN	TIME OUT

Bar/psi START	Bar/psi END

| SI | PG | | PG |

☐ Computer Dive

Bottom Time

Depth

RNT _________
ABT _________
TBT _________

VISIBILITY

____

TEMP: Air _______ Surface _______ Bottom _______

GEAR USED

BCD: ___________________

Wetsuit: _______________

Fins: __________________

Weights: _____________ kg/lbs

Cylinder: _____________ liters

DIVE SHOP STAMP

☐ Steel   ☐ Aluminum

☐ Fresh   ☐ Salt   ☐ Shore   ☐ Boat   ☐ Drift   ☐ Night   ☐ Training

DIVE COMMENTS

____

____

____

____

____

____

Bottom Time to Date: ___________

Time of this Dive: ______________

Cumulative Dive Time: ___________

Verification Signature

____

☐ Instructor   ☐ Divemaster   ☐ Buddy

Certification No: __________

Dive Number: _______________________

Date: _______________________

Location: _______________________

Ocean: _______________________

TIME IN	TIME OUT

Bar/psi START	Bar/psi END

SI	PG		PG

☐ Computer Dive

Bottom Time

Depth

RNT _______
ABT _______
TBT _______

VISIBILITY
____

TEMP: Air _______ Surface _______ Bottom _______

GEAR USED

BCD: _______________

Wetsuit: _____________

Fins: _______________

Weights: _____________ kg/lbs

Cylinder: _____________ liters

DIVE SHOP STAMP

☐ Steel   ☐ Aluminum

☐ Fresh   ☐ Salt   ☐ Shore   ☐ Boat   ☐ Drift   ☐ Night   ☐ Training

DIVE COMMENTS

____

____

____

____

____

____

Bottom Time to Date: ____________

Time of this Dive: ______________

Cumulative Dive Time: ____________

Verification Signature

____

☐ Instructor   ☐ Divemaster   ☐ Buddy

Certification No: _________

Dive Number: _______________________

Date: _______________________________

Location: ____________________________

Ocean: ______________________________

TIME IN	TIME OUT

Bar/psi START	Bar/psi END

| SI | PG | | PG |

☐ Computer Dive

Bottom Time

Depth

RNT _______
ABT _______
TBT _______

VISIBILITY
____

TEMP: Air ______ Surface _______ Bottom ______

GEAR USED

BCD: __________________

Wetsuit: ______________

Fins: _________________

Weights: ______________ kg/lbs

Cylinder: _____________ liters

DIVE SHOP STAMP

☐ Steel   ☐ Aluminum

☐ Fresh   ☐ Salt   ☐ Shore   ☐ Boat   ☐ Drift   ☐ Night   ☐ Training

DIVE COMMENTS

____

____

____

____

____

Bottom Time to Date: ____________

Time of this Dive: ______________

Cumulative Dive Time: ___________

Verification Signature

____

☐ Instructor   ☐ Divemaster   ☐ Buddy

Certification No: __________

Dive Number: ___________________

Date: ___________________

Location: ___________________

Ocean: ___________________

TIME IN	TIME OUT

Bar/psi START	Bar/psi END

| SI | PG | | PG |

☐ Computer Dive

Bottom Time

Depth

RNT ________
ABT ________
TBT ________

VISIBILITY
____

TEMP: Air ________ Surface ________ Bottom ________

GEAR USED

BCD: ___________________

Wetsuit: ___________________

Fins: ___________________

Weights: ___________________ kg/lbs

Cylinder: ___________________ liters

DIVE SHOP STAMP

☐ Steel   ☐ Aluminum

☐ Fresh   ☐ Salt   ☐ Shore   ☐ Boat   ☐ Drift   ☐ Night   ☐ Training

DIVE COMMENTS

____

____

____

____

____

____

Bottom Time to Date: ___________

Time of this Dive: ___________

Cumulative Dive Time: ___________

Verification Signature

____

☐ Instructor   ☐ Divemaster   ☐ Buddy

Certification No: ___________

Dive Number: _____________________

Date: ___________________________

Location: _______________________

Ocean: _________________________

TIME IN	TIME OUT

Bar/psi
START

Bar/psi
END

SI	PG		PG

☐ Computer
Dive

Bottom Time

Depth

RNT _______
ABT _______
TBT _______

VISIBILITY
____

TEMP: Air ______ Surface ______ Bottom ______

GEAR USED

BCD: __________________

Wetsuit: ______________

Fins: _________________

Weights: _____________ kg/lbs

Cylinder: _____________ liters

DIVE SHOP STAMP

☐ Steel ☐ Aluminum

☐ Fresh ☐ Salt ☐ Shore ☐ Boat ☐ Drift ☐ Night ☐ Training

DIVE COMMENTS

____

____

____

____

____

____

Bottom Time to Date: ___________

Time of this Dive: _____________

Cumulative Dive Time: ___________

Verification Signature

____

☐ Instructor ☐ Divemaster ☐ Buddy

Certification No: ___________

Dive Number: _______________

Date: _______________

Location: _______________

Ocean: _______________

TIME IN	TIME OUT

Bar/psi START	Bar/psi END

SI | PG

PG

☐ Computer Dive

Bottom Time

Depth

RNT _______
ABT _______
TBT _______

VISIBILITY
____

TEMP: Air _______ Surface _______ Bottom _______

GEAR USED

BCD: _______________
Wetsuit: _______________
Fins: _______________
Weights: _______________ kg/lbs
Cylinder: _______________ liters

DIVE SHOP STAMP

☐ Steel ☐ Aluminum

☐ Fresh ☐ Salt ☐ Shore ☐ Boat ☐ Drift ☐ Night ☐ Training

DIVE COMMENTS

____

____

____

____

____

____

Bottom Time to Date: _______________

Time of this Dive: _______________

Cumulative Dive Time: _______________

Verification Signature

____

☐ Instructor ☐ Divemaster ☐ Buddy

Certification No: _______________

Dive Number: _________________

Date: ___________________________

Location: _______________________

Ocean: _________________________

TIME IN	TIME OUT

Bar/psi START	Bar/psi END

SI	PG		PG

☐ Computer Dive

Bottom Time

Depth

RNT ________
ABT ________
TBT ________

VISIBILITY

____

TEMP: Air ______ Surface ______ Bottom ______

GEAR USED

BCD: _________________

Wetsuit: ______________

Fins: _________________

Weights: _____________ kg/lbs

Cylinder: ____________ liters

DIVE SHOP STAMP

☐ Steel ☐ Aluminum

☐ Fresh ☐ Salt ☐ Shore ☐ Boat ☐ Drift ☐ Night ☐ Training

DIVE COMMENTS

____

____

____

____

____

____

Bottom Time to Date: ___________

Time of this Dive: _____________

Cumulative Dive Time: ___________

Verification Signature

____

☐ Instructor ☐ Divemaster ☐ Buddy

Certification No: _________

Dive Number: _______________________

Date: _______________________

Location: _______________________

Ocean: _______________________

TIME IN	TIME OUT

SI	PG		PG

☐ Computer Dive

Bottom Time

Depth

Bar/psi START	Bar/psi END

RNT ______
ABT ______
TBT ______

VISIBILITY
____

TEMP: Air ______ Surface ______ Bottom ______

GEAR USED

BCD: _______________________

Wetsuit: _______________________

Fins: _______________________

Weights: _______________________ kg/lbs

Cylinder: _______________________ liters

DIVE SHOP STAMP

☐ Steel ☐ Aluminum

☐ Fresh ☐ Salt ☐ Shore ☐ Boat ☐ Drift ☐ Night ☐ Training

DIVE COMMENTS

____

____

____

____

____

____

Bottom Time to Date: _______________

Time of this Dive: _______________

Cumulative Dive Time: _______________

Verification Signature

____

☐ Instructor ☐ Divemaster ☐ Buddy

Certification No: _______________

Dive Number: _____________________

Date: _____________________

Location: _____________________

Ocean: _____________________

TIME IN	TIME OUT

Bar/psi START	Bar/psi END

SI | PG | PG

☐ Computer Dive

Bottom Time

Depth

RNT _______
ABT _______
TBT _______

VISIBILITY
____

TEMP: Air _______ Surface _______ Bottom _______

GEAR USED

BCD: _____________________

Wetsuit: _____________________

Fins: _____________________

Weights: _____________________ kg/lbs

Cylinder: _____________________ liters

DIVE SHOP STAMP

☐ Steel   ☐ Aluminum

☐ Fresh   ☐ Salt   ☐ Shore   ☐ Boat   ☐ Drift   ☐ Night   ☐ Training

DIVE COMMENTS

____

____

____

____

____

____

Bottom Time to Date: _____________

Time of this Dive: _______________

Cumulative Dive Time: ___________

Verification Signature

____

☐ Instructor   ☐ Divemaster   ☐ Buddy

Certification No: __________

Dive Number: _______________________

Date: ____________________________

Location: _________________________

Ocean: ___________________________

TIME IN	TIME OUT

Bar/psi START	Bar/psi END

SI	PG		PG

☐ Computer Dive

Bottom Time

Depth

RNT _______
ABT _______
TBT _______

VISIBILITY
____

TEMP: Air _______ Surface _______ Bottom _______

GEAR USED

BCD: _________________

Wetsuit: ______________

Fins: _________________

Weights: ______________ kg/lbs

Cylinder: ______________ liters

DIVE SHOP STAMP

☐ Steel   ☐ Aluminum

☐ Fresh   ☐ Salt   ☐ Shore   ☐ Boat   ☐ Drift   ☐ Night   ☐ Training

DIVE COMMENTS

____

____

____

____

____

____

Bottom Time to Date: ___________

Time of this Dive: _____________

Cumulative Dive Time: ___________

Verification Signature

____

☐ Instructor   ☐ Divemaster   ☐ Buddy

Certification No: _________

Dive Number: ___________________
Date: _______________________
Location: _____________________
Ocean: ______________________

TIME IN	TIME OUT

Bar/psi START	Bar/psi END

☐ Computer Dive

Bottom Time

Depth

SI | PG | PG

RNT _______
ABT _______
TBT _______

VISIBILITY

____

TEMP: Air _______ Surface _______ Bottom _______

DIVE SHOP STAMP

GEAR USED

BCD: _______________
Wetsuit: _____________
Fins: _______________
Weights: _____________ kg/lbs
Cylinder: ___________ liters

☐ Steel   ☐ Aluminum

☐ Fresh   ☐ Salt   ☐ Shore   ☐ Boat   ☐ Drift   ☐ Night   ☐ Training

DIVE COMMENTS

____
____
____
____
____
____

Bottom Time to Date: ___________

Time of this Dive: _____________

Cumulative Dive Time: ___________

Verification Signature

____

☐ Instructor   ☐ Divemaster   ☐ Buddy

Certification No: _________

Dive Number: ___________________
Date: ___________________
Location: ___________________
Ocean: ___________________

TIME IN	TIME OUT

Bar/psi START	Bar/psi END

		PG
SI	PG	

☐ Computer Dive

Bottom Time

Depth

RNT _______
ABT _______
TBT _______

VISIBILITY
____

TEMP: Air _______ Surface _______ Bottom _______

DIVE SHOP STAMP

GEAR USED

BCD: ___________________
Wetsuit: ___________________
Fins: ___________________
Weights: ___________________ kg/lbs
Cylinder: ___________________ liters

☐ Steel   ☐ Aluminum

☐ Fresh   ☐ Salt   ☐ Shore   ☐ Boat   ☐ Drift   ☐ Night   ☐ Training

DIVE COMMENTS

____
____
____
____
____
____

Bottom Time to Date: ___________

Time of this Dive: ___________

Cumulative Dive Time: ___________

Verification Signature

____

☐ Instructor   ☐ Divemaster   ☐ Buddy

Certification No: ___________

Dive Number: ______________________

Date: ______________________

Location: ______________________

Ocean: ______________________

TIME IN	TIME OUT

Bar/psi START	Bar/psi END

SI	PG		PG

☐ Computer Dive

Bottom Time

Depth

RNT _______
ABT _______
TBT _______

VISIBILITY
____

TEMP: Air _______ Surface _______ Bottom _______

GEAR USED

BCD: ______________________

Wetsuit: ______________________

Fins: ______________________

Weights: ______________________ kg/lbs

Cylinder: ______________________ liters

DIVE SHOP STAMP

☐ Steel ☐ Aluminum

☐ Fresh ☐ Salt ☐ Shore ☐ Boat ☐ Drift ☐ Night ☐ Training

DIVE COMMENTS

____

____

____

____

____

____

Bottom Time to Date: ______________

Time of this Dive: ______________

Cumulative Dive Time: ______________

Verification Signature

____

☐ Instructor ☐ Divemaster ☐ Buddy

Certification No: ______________

Dive Number: _______________

Date: _________________________

Location: ______________________

Ocean: _________________________

TIME IN	TIME OUT

Bar/psi START	Bar/psi END

SI	PG		PG

☐ Computer Dive

Bottom Time

Depth

RNT _______
ABT _______
TBT _______

VISIBILITY
____

TEMP: Air _______ Surface _______ Bottom _______

GEAR USED

BCD: _________________

Wetsuit: _____________

Fins: _________________

Weights: _____________ kg/lbs

Cylinder: _____________ liters

DIVE SHOP STAMP

☐ Steel   ☐ Aluminum

☐ Fresh   ☐ Salt   ☐ Shore   ☐ Boat   ☐ Drift   ☐ Night   ☐ Training

DIVE COMMENTS

____

____

____

____

____

____

Bottom Time to Date: ___________

Time of this Dive: _____________

Cumulative Dive Time: ___________

Verification Signature

____

☐ Instructor   ☐ Divemaster   ☐ Buddy

Certification No: _________

Dive Number: _______________________

Date: _____________________________

Location: _________________________

Ocean: ____________________________

TIME IN	TIME OUT

Bar/psi START	Bar/psi END

SI	PG		PG

☐ Computer Dive

Bottom Time

Depth

RNT ________
ABT ________
TBT ________

VISIBILITY
____

TEMP: Air ______ Surface ______ Bottom ______

GEAR USED

BCD: _________________

Wetsuit: _____________

Fins: ________________

Weights: _____________ kg/lbs

Cylinder: ____________ liters

DIVE SHOP STAMP

☐ Steel   ☐ Aluminum

☐ Fresh   ☐ Salt   ☐ Shore   ☐ Boat   ☐ Drift   ☐ Night   ☐ Training

DIVE COMMENTS

____

____

____

____

____

____

Bottom Time to Date: ___________

Time of this Dive: _____________

Cumulative Dive Time: ___________

Verification Signature

____

☐ Instructor   ☐ Divemaster   ☐ Buddy

Certification No: _________

Dive Number: ________________

Date: ___________________

Location: _________________

Ocean: ___________________

TIME IN	TIME OUT

Bar/psi START	Bar/psi END

| SI | PG | | PG |

☐ Computer Dive

Bottom Time

Depth

RNT ________
ABT ________
TBT ________

VISIBILITY
____

TEMP: Air ______ Surface ______ Bottom ______

GEAR USED

BCD: _________________

Wetsuit: _____________

Fins: ________________

Weights: ____________ kg/lbs

Cylinder: ____________ liters

DIVE SHOP STAMP

☐ Steel ☐ Aluminum

☐ Fresh ☐ Salt ☐ Shore ☐ Boat ☐ Drift ☐ Night ☐ Training

DIVE COMMENTS

____

____

____

____

____

____

Bottom Time to Date: ___________

Time of this Dive: ______________

Cumulative Dive Time: ___________

Verification Signature

____

☐ Instructor ☐ Divemaster ☐ Buddy

Certification No: _________

Dive Number: _______________

Date: _______________

Location: _______________

Ocean: _______________

SI	PG		PG

☐ Computer Dive

Bottom Time

Depth

TIME IN	**TIME OUT**

Bar/psi START	Bar/psi END

RNT _______
ABT _______
TBT _______

VISIBILITY

____

TEMP: Air _______ Surface _______ Bottom _______

GEAR USED

BCD: _______________

Wetsuit: _______________

Fins: _______________

Weights: _______________ kg/lbs

Cylinder: _______________ liters

DIVE SHOP STAMP

☐ Steel   ☐ Aluminum

☐ Fresh   ☐ Salt   ☐ Shore   ☐ Boat   ☐ Drift   ☐ Night   ☐ Training

DIVE COMMENTS

____

____

____

____

____

____

Bottom Time to Date: _______________

Time of this Dive: _______________

Cumulative Dive Time: _______________

Verification Signature

____

☐ Instructor   ☐ Divemaster   ☐ Buddy

Certification No: _______________

Dive Number: ______________________
Date: ______________________
Location: ______________________
Ocean: ______________________

TIME IN	TIME OUT

SI	PG	PG

☐ Computer Dive

Bottom Time

Depth

Bar/psi START	Bar/psi END

RNT ______
ABT ______
TBT ______

VISIBILITY
____

TEMP: Air ______ Surface ______ Bottom ______

GEAR USED

BCD: ______________________
Wetsuit: ______________________
Fins: ______________________
Weights: ______________________ kg/lbs
Cylinder: ______________________ liters

DIVE SHOP STAMP

☐ Steel   ☐ Aluminum

☐ Fresh   ☐ Salt   ☐ Shore   ☐ Boat   ☐ Drift   ☐ Night   ☐ Training

DIVE COMMENTS

____
____
____
____
____
____

Bottom Time to Date: ______________

Time of this Dive: ______________

Cumulative Dive Time: ______________

Verification Signature

____

☐ Instructor   ☐ Divemaster   ☐ Buddy

Certification No: ______________

Dive Number: ______________________

Date: ______________________

Location: ______________________

Ocean: ______________________

TIME IN	TIME OUT

Bar/psi START	Bar/psi END

SI	PG		PG

☐ Computer Dive

Bottom Time

Depth

RNT ________
ABT ________
TBT ________

VISIBILITY
____

TEMP: Air ______ Surface ______ Bottom ______

GEAR USED

BCD: ______________________

Wetsuit: ______________________

Fins: ______________________

Weights: ______________________ kg/lbs

Cylinder: ______________________ liters

DIVE SHOP STAMP

☐ Steel   ☐ Aluminum

☐ Fresh   ☐ Salt   ☐ Shore   ☐ Boat   ☐ Drift   ☐ Night   ☐ Training

DIVE COMMENTS

____

____

____

____

____

____

Bottom Time to Date: ______________

Time of this Dive: ______________

Cumulative Dive Time: ______________

Verification Signature

____

☐ Instructor   ☐ Divemaster   ☐ Buddy

Certification No: ______________

Dive Number: ___________________

Date: _______________________________

Location: _____________________________

Ocean: _______________________________

TIME IN	TIME OUT

Bar/psi START	Bar/psi END

SI | PG | PG

☐ Computer Dive

Bottom Time

Depth

RNT _______
ABT _______
TBT _______

VISIBILITY
____

TEMP: Air ______ Surface ______ Bottom ______

GEAR USED

BCD: __________________

Wetsuit: ______________

Fins: __________________

Weights: _____________ kg/lbs

Cylinder: _____________ liters

DIVE SHOP STAMP

☐ Steel ☐ Aluminum

☐ Fresh ☐ Salt ☐ Shore ☐ Boat ☐ Drift ☐ Night ☐ Training

DIVE COMMENTS

____

____

____

____

____

____

Bottom Time to Date: ____________

Time of this Dive: _______________

Cumulative Dive Time: ____________

Verification Signature

____

☐ Instructor   ☐ Divemaster   ☐ Buddy

Certification No: __________

Dive Number: _______________

Date: _______________

Location: _______________

Ocean: _______________

TIME IN	TIME OUT

Bar/psi START	Bar/psi END

| SI | PG | | PG |

☐ Computer Dive

Bottom Time

Depth

RNT _______
ABT _______
TBT _______

VISIBILITY
____

TEMP: Air _______ Surface _______ Bottom _______

GEAR USED

BCD: _______________
Wetsuit: _______________
Fins: _______________
Weights: _______________ kg/lbs
Cylinder: _______________ liters

DIVE SHOP STAMP

☐ Steel ☐ Aluminum

☐ Fresh ☐ Salt ☐ Shore ☐ Boat ☐ Drift ☐ Night ☐ Training

DIVE COMMENTS

____
____
____
____
____
____

Bottom Time to Date: _______________

Time of this Dive: _______________

Cumulative Dive Time: _______________

Verification Signature

____

☐ Instructor ☐ Divemaster ☐ Buddy

Certification No: _______________

Dive Number: _______________________

Date: _______________________

Location: _______________________

Ocean: _______________________

TIME IN	TIME OUT

Bar/psi START	Bar/psi END

SI | PG | PG

☐ Computer Dive

Bottom Time

Depth

RNT _______
ABT _______
TBT _______

VISIBILITY
____

TEMP: Air _______ Surface _______ Bottom _______

GEAR USED

BCD: _______________

Wetsuit: _______________

Fins: _______________

Weights: _______________ kg/lbs

Cylinder: _______________ liters

DIVE SHOP STAMP

☐ Steel   ☐ Aluminum

☐ Fresh   ☐ Salt   ☐ Shore   ☐ Boat   ☐ Drift   ☐ Night   ☐ Training

DIVE COMMENTS

____

____

____

____

____

____

Bottom Time to Date: _______________

Time of this Dive: _______________

Cumulative Dive Time: _______________

Verification Signature

____

☐ Instructor   ☐ Divemaster   ☐ Buddy

Certification No: _______________

Dive Number: _______________________

Date: _______________________

Location: _______________________

Ocean: _______________________

TIME IN	TIME OUT

Bar/psi START	Bar/psi END

SI	PG		PG

☐ Computer Dive

Bottom Time

Depth

RNT _______
ABT _______
TBT _______

VISIBILITY
____

TEMP: Air _______ Surface _______ Bottom _______

GEAR USED

BCD: _______________

Wetsuit: _____________

Fins: ________________

Weights: _____________ kg/lbs

Cylinder: _____________ liters

DIVE SHOP STAMP

☐ Steel   ☐ Aluminum

☐ Fresh   ☐ Salt   ☐ Shore   ☐ Boat   ☐ Drift   ☐ Night   ☐ Training

DIVE COMMENTS

____

____

____

____

____

____

Bottom Time to Date: ___________

Time of this Dive: _____________

Cumulative Dive Time: ___________

Verification Signature

____

☐ Instructor   ☐ Divemaster   ☐ Buddy

Certification No: _________

Dive Number: _______________________

Date: _________________________________

Location: ____________________________

Ocean: _______________________________

TIME IN	TIME OUT

Bar/psi START	Bar/psi END

	SI	PG			PG

☐ Computer Dive

Bottom Time

Depth

RNT _______
ABT _______
TBT _______

VISIBILITY

____

TEMP: Air _______ Surface _______ Bottom _______

GEAR USED

BCD: ___________________

Wetsuit: _______________

Fins: __________________

Weights: _______________ kg/lbs

Cylinder: ______________ liters

DIVE SHOP STAMP

☐ Steel   ☐ Aluminum

☐ Fresh   ☐ Salt   ☐ Shore   ☐ Boat   ☐ Drift   ☐ Night   ☐ Training

DIVE COMMENTS

____

____

____

____

____

____

Bottom Time to Date: ____________

Time of this Dive: _______________

Cumulative Dive Time: ___________

Verification Signature

____

☐ Instructor   ☐ Divemaster   ☐ Buddy

Certification No: __________

Dive Number: ________________

Date: ________________

Location: ________________

Ocean: ________________

TIME IN	TIME OUT

Bar/psi START	Bar/psi END

SI	PG		PG

☐ Computer Dive

Bottom Time

Depth

RNT ________
ABT ________
TBT ________

VISIBILITY

____

TEMP: Air ________ Surface ________ Bottom ________

GEAR USED

BCD: ________________

Wetsuit: ________________

Fins: ________________

Weights: ________________ kg/lbs

Cylinder: ________________ liters

DIVE SHOP STAMP

☐ Steel   ☐ Aluminum

☐ Fresh   ☐ Salt   ☐ Shore   ☐ Boat   ☐ Drift   ☐ Night   ☐ Training

DIVE COMMENTS

____

____

____

____

____

____

Bottom Time to Date: ________________

Time of this Dive: ________________

Cumulative Dive Time: ________________

Verification Signature

____

☐ Instructor   ☐ Divemaster   ☐ Buddy

Certification No: ________________

Dive Number: _____________________

Date: _____________________

Location: _____________________

Ocean: _____________________

TIME IN	TIME OUT

Bar/psi START	Bar/psi END

SI	PG		PG

☐ Computer Dive

Bottom Time

Depth

RNT _______
ABT _______
TBT _______

VISIBILITY
____

TEMP: Air ______ Surface ______ Bottom ______

GEAR USED

BCD: _____________________

Wetsuit: _____________________

Fins: _____________________

Weights: _____________ kg/lbs

Cylinder: _____________ liters

DIVE SHOP STAMP

☐ Steel   ☐ Aluminum

☐ Fresh   ☐ Salt   ☐ Shore   ☐ Boat   ☐ Drift   ☐ Night   ☐ Training

DIVE COMMENTS

____

____

____

____

____

____

Bottom Time to Date: _____________

Time of this Dive: _____________

Cumulative Dive Time: _____________

Verification Signature

____

☐ Instructor   ☐ Divemaster   ☐ Buddy

Certification No: _____________

Dive Number: ______________________

Date: ______________________

Location: ______________________

Ocean: ______________________

TIME IN	TIME OUT

Bar/psi
START

Bar/psi
END

SI	PG		PG

☐ Computer Dive

Bottom Time

Depth

RNT ______
ABT ______
TBT ______

VISIBILITY

____

TEMP: Air ______ Surface ______ Bottom ______

GEAR USED

BCD: ______________

Wetsuit: ______________

Fins: ______________

Weights: ______________ kg/lbs

Cylinder: ______________ liters

DIVE SHOP STAMP

☐ Steel   ☐ Aluminum

☐ Fresh   ☐ Salt   ☐ Shore   ☐ Boat   ☐ Drift   ☐ Night   ☐ Training

DIVE COMMENTS

____

____

____

____

____

____

Bottom Time to Date: ______________

Time of this Dive: ______________

Cumulative Dive Time: ______________

Verification Signature

____

☐ Instructor   ☐ Divemaster   ☐ Buddy

Certification No: ______________

Dive Number: _________________

Date: _________________________

Location: ______________________

Ocean: _________________________

TIME IN	TIME OUT

Bar/psi START	Bar/psi END

SI | PG | PG

☐ Computer Dive

Bottom Time

Depth

RNT ________
ABT ________
TBT ________

VISIBILITY
____

TEMP: Air ______ Surface ______ Bottom ______

GEAR USED

BCD: __________________

Wetsuit: ____________

Fins: ________________

Weights: ____________ kg/lbs

Cylinder: ____________ liters

DIVE SHOP STAMP

☐ Steel   ☐ Aluminum

☐ Fresh   ☐ Salt   ☐ Shore   ☐ Boat   ☐ Drift   ☐ Night   ☐ Training

DIVE COMMENTS

____

____

____

____

____

____

Bottom Time to Date: ___________

Time of this Dive: _____________

Cumulative Dive Time: __________

Verification Signature

____

☐ Instructor   ☐ Divemaster   ☐ Buddy

Certification No: _________

Dive Number: _______________

Date: _______________

Location: _______________

Ocean: _______________

TIME IN	TIME OUT

Bar/psi START	Bar/psi END

| SI | PG | | PG |

☐ Computer Dive

Bottom Time

Depth

RNT _______
ABT _______
TBT _______

VISIBILITY
____

TEMP: Air _______ Surface _______ Bottom _______

GEAR USED

BCD: _______________
Wetsuit: _______________
Fins: _______________
Weights: _______________ kg/lbs
Cylinder: _______________ liters

DIVE SHOP STAMP

☐ Steel   ☐ Aluminum

☐ Fresh   ☐ Salt   ☐ Shore   ☐ Boat   ☐ Drift   ☐ Night   ☐ Training

DIVE COMMENTS

____

____

____

____

____

____

Bottom Time to Date: _______________

Time of this Dive: _______________

Cumulative Dive Time: _______________

Verification Signature

____

☐ Instructor   ☐ Divemaster   ☐ Buddy

Certification No: _______________

Dive Number: ___________________

Date: _______________________

Location: ____________________

Ocean: _______________________

TIME IN	TIME OUT

Bar/psi START	Bar/psi END

☐ Computer Dive

| SI | PG | | PG |

Bottom Time

Depth

RNT _______
ABT _______
TBT _______

VISIBILITY
____

TEMP: Air ______ Surface ______ Bottom ______

GEAR USED

BCD: ___________________

Wetsuit: _______________

Fins: __________________

Weights: ______________ kg/lbs

Cylinder: ____________ liters

DIVE SHOP STAMP

☐ Steel ☐ Aluminum

☐ Fresh ☐ Salt ☐ Shore ☐ Boat ☐ Drift ☐ Night ☐ Training

DIVE COMMENTS

____

____

____

____

____

____

Bottom Time to Date: ___________

Time of this Dive: ___________

Cumulative Dive Time: ___________

Verification Signature

____

☐ Instructor   ☐ Divemaster   ☐ Buddy

Certification No: __________

Dive Number: ___________________
Date: ___________________
Location: ___________________
Ocean: ___________________

TIME IN	TIME OUT

Bar/psi START	Bar/psi END

SI	PG		PG

☐ Computer Dive

Bottom Time

Depth

RNT ________
ABT ________
TBT ________

VISIBILITY
____

TEMP: Air ______ Surface ______ Bottom ______

GEAR USED

BCD: ___________________
Wetsuit: ___________________
Fins: ___________________
Weights: ___________________ kg/lbs
Cylinder: ___________________ liters

DIVE SHOP STAMP

☐ Steel   ☐ Aluminum

☐ Fresh   ☐ Salt   ☐ Shore   ☐ Boat   ☐ Drift   ☐ Night   ☐ Training

DIVE COMMENTS

____
____
____
____
____
____

Bottom Time to Date: ___________

Time of this Dive: ___________

Cumulative Dive Time: ___________

Verification Signature

____

☐ Instructor   ☐ Divemaster   ☐ Buddy

Certification No: ___________

Dive Number: _______________

Date: _________________________

Location: ___________________

Ocean: _____________________

TIME IN	TIME OUT

Bar/psi START	Bar/psi END

SI | PG | PG

☐ Computer Dive

Bottom Time

Depth

RNT _______
ABT _______
TBT _______

VISIBILITY

____

TEMP: Air _______ Surface _______ Bottom _______

GEAR USED

BCD: _________________

Wetsuit: ______________

Fins: _________________

Weights: _____________ kg/lbs

Cylinder: _____________ liters

DIVE SHOP STAMP

☐ Steel ☐ Aluminum

☐ Fresh ☐ Salt ☐ Shore ☐ Boat ☐ Drift ☐ Night ☐ Training

DIVE COMMENTS

____

____

____

____

____

____

Bottom Time to Date: ___________

Time of this Dive: _____________

Cumulative Dive Time: ___________

Verification Signature

____

☐ Instructor ☐ Divemaster ☐ Buddy

Certification No: _________

Dive Number: _______________________

Date: _______________________

Location: _______________________

Ocean: _______________________

TIME IN	TIME OUT

Bar/psi START	Bar/psi END

SI	PG		PG

☐ Computer Dive

Bottom Time

Depth

RNT _______
ABT _______
TBT _______

VISIBILITY
____

TEMP: Air _______ Surface _______ Bottom _______

DIVE SHOP STAMP

GEAR USED

BCD: _______________

Wetsuit: _______________

Fins: _______________

Weights: _______________ kg/lbs

Cylinder: _______________ liters

☐ Steel   ☐ Aluminum

☐ Fresh   ☐ Salt   ☐ Shore   ☐ Boat   ☐ Drift   ☐ Night   ☐ Training

DIVE COMMENTS

____

____

____

____

____

____

Bottom Time to Date: _______________

Time of this Dive: _______________

Cumulative Dive Time: _______________

Verification Signature

____

☐ Instructor   ☐ Divemaster   ☐ Buddy

Certification No: _______________

Dive Number: _______________

Date: _____________________

Location: __________________

Ocean: ____________________

TIME IN	TIME OUT

Bar/psi START	Bar/psi END

☐ Computer Dive

SI | PG | PG

Bottom Time

Depth

RNT _______
ABT _______
TBT _______

VISIBILITY
____

TEMP: Air _______ Surface _______ Bottom _______

GEAR USED

BCD: _________________

Wetsuit: ______________

Fins: ________________

Weights: ____________ kg/lbs

Cylinder: ____________ liters

DIVE SHOP STAMP

☐ Steel   ☐ Aluminum

☐ Fresh   ☐ Salt   ☐ Shore   ☐ Boat   ☐ Drift   ☐ Night   ☐ Training

DIVE COMMENTS

____

____

____

____

____

____

Bottom Time to Date: ___________

Time of this Dive: ______________

Cumulative Dive Time: ___________

Verification Signature

____

☐ Instructor   ☐ Divemaster   ☐ Buddy

Certification No: __________

Dive Number: ___________________

Date: _______________________

Location: _____________________

Ocean: _______________________

TIME IN	TIME OUT

Bar/psi START	Bar/psi END

SI	PG		PG

☐ Computer Dive

Bottom Time

Depth

RNT _______
ABT _______
TBT _______

VISIBILITY
____

TEMP: Air _______   Surface _______   Bottom _______

GEAR USED

BCD: ________________

Wetsuit: ____________

Fins: ________________

Weights: ____________ kg/lbs

Cylinder: ____________ liters

DIVE SHOP STAMP

☐ Steel   ☐ Aluminum

☐ Fresh   ☐ Salt   ☐ Shore   ☐ Boat   ☐ Drift   ☐ Night   ☐ Training

DIVE COMMENTS

____

____

____

____

____

____

Bottom Time to Date: ___________

Time of this Dive: _____________

Cumulative Dive Time: ___________

Verification Signature

____

☐ Instructor   ☐ Divemaster   ☐ Buddy

Certification No: _________

Dive Number: ___________________

Date: _____________________________

Location: _________________________

Ocean: ____________________________

TIME IN	TIME OUT

Bar/psi START	Bar/psi END

SI	PG		PG

☐ Computer Dive

Bottom Time

Depth

RNT ________
ABT ________
TBT ________

VISIBILITY
____

TEMP: Air ______   Surface ______   Bottom ______

GEAR USED

BCD: _________________

Wetsuit: ____________

Fins: ________________

Weights: _____________ kg/lbs

Cylinder: _____________ liters

DIVE SHOP STAMP

☐ Steel   ☐ Aluminum

☐ Fresh   ☐ Salt   ☐ Shore   ☐ Boat   ☐ Drift   ☐ Night   ☐ Training

DIVE COMMENTS

____

____

____

____

____

Bottom Time to Date: ___________

Time of this Dive: _____________

Cumulative Dive Time: __________

Verification Signature

____

☐ Instructor   ☐ Divemaster   ☐ Buddy

Certification No: _________

Dive Number: _________________

Date: _____________________

Location: ___________________

Ocean: _____________________

TIME IN	TIME OUT

Bar/psi START	Bar/psi END

| SI | PG | | PG |

☐ Computer Dive

Bottom Time

Depth

RNT _______
ABT _______
TBT _______

VISIBILITY
____

TEMP: Air ______ Surface ______ Bottom ______

GEAR USED

BCD: _________________
Wetsuit: ______________
Fins: ________________
Weights: _____________ kg/lbs
Cylinder: _____________ liters

DIVE SHOP STAMP

☐ Steel   ☐ Aluminum

☐ Fresh   ☐ Salt   ☐ Shore   ☐ Boat   ☐ Drift   ☐ Night   ☐ Training

DIVE COMMENTS

____

____

____

____

____

____

Bottom Time to Date: ___________

Time of this Dive: _____________

Cumulative Dive Time: __________

Verification Signature

____

☐ Instructor   ☐ Divemaster   ☐ Buddy

Certification No: _________

Dive Number: ___________________
Date: ____________________________
Location: _________________________
Ocean: ___________________________

TIME IN	TIME OUT

Bar/psi START	Bar/psi END

<table><tr><td>SI</td><td>PG</td><td></td><td>PG</td></tr></table>

☐ Computer Dive

Bottom Time

Depth

RNT ________
ABT ________
TBT ________

VISIBILITY
____

TEMP: Air ______ Surface ______ Bottom ______

GEAR USED

BCD: _________________
Wetsuit: ____________
Fins: _________________
Weights: ____________ kg/lbs
Cylinder: ____________ liters

DIVE SHOP STAMP

☐ Steel   ☐ Aluminum

☐ Fresh   ☐ Salt   ☐ Shore   ☐ Boat   ☐ Drift   ☐ Night   ☐ Training

DIVE COMMENTS

____
____
____
____
____
____

Bottom Time to Date: ___________

Time of this Dive: _______________

Cumulative Dive Time: ___________

Verification Signature

____

☐ Instructor   ☐ Divemaster   ☐ Buddy

Certification No: __________

Dive Number: ______________________

Date: ______________________

Location: ______________________

Ocean: ______________________

TIME IN	TIME OUT

Bar/psi
START

Bar/psi
END

SI | PG | PG

☐ Computer Dive

Bottom Time

Depth

RNT ______
ABT ______
TBT ______

VISIBILITY
____

TEMP: Air ______ Surface ______ Bottom ______

GEAR USED

BCD: ______________

Wetsuit: ______________

Fins: ______________

Weights: ______________ kg/lbs

Cylinder: ______________ liters

DIVE SHOP STAMP

☐ Steel   ☐ Aluminum

☐ Fresh   ☐ Salt   ☐ Shore   ☐ Boat   ☐ Drift   ☐ Night   ☐ Training

DIVE COMMENTS

____

____

____

____

____

____

Bottom Time to Date: ______________

Time of this Dive: ______________

Cumulative Dive Time: ______________

Verification Signature

____

☐ Instructor   ☐ Divemaster   ☐ Buddy

Certification No: ______________

Dive Number: _________________

Date: _________________

Location: _________________

Ocean: _________________

TIME IN	TIME OUT

Bar/psi START	Bar/psi END

SI | PG | PG

☐ Computer Dive

Bottom Time

Depth

RNT _______
ABT _______
TBT _______

VISIBILITY

____

TEMP: Air ______ Surface ______ Bottom ______

GEAR USED

BCD: _________________
Wetsuit: _________________
Fins: _________________
Weights: _________________ kg/lbs
Cylinder: _________________ liters

DIVE SHOP STAMP

☐ Steel ☐ Aluminum

☐ Fresh ☐ Salt ☐ Shore ☐ Boat ☐ Drift ☐ Night ☐ Training

DIVE COMMENTS

____

____

____

____

____

____

Bottom Time to Date: _________

Time of this Dive: _________

Cumulative Dive Time: _________

Verification Signature

____

☐ Instructor ☐ Divemaster ☐ Buddy

Certification No: _________

Dive Number: ___________________
Date: ___________________
Location: ___________________
Ocean: ___________________

TIME IN	TIME OUT

Bar/psi START	Bar/psi END

| SI | PG | | PG |

☐ Computer Dive

Bottom Time

Depth

RNT ________
ABT ________
TBT ________

VISIBILITY
____

TEMP: Air ________ Surface ________ Bottom ________

GEAR USED

BCD: ___________________
Wetsuit: ___________________
Fins: ___________________
Weights: ___________________ kg/lbs
Cylinder: ___________________ liters

DIVE SHOP STAMP

☐ Steel   ☐ Aluminum

☐ Fresh   ☐ Salt   ☐ Shore   ☐ Boat   ☐ Drift   ☐ Night   ☐ Training

DIVE COMMENTS

____
____
____
____
____
____

Bottom Time to Date: ___________

Time of this Dive: ___________

Cumulative Dive Time: ___________

Verification Signature

____

☐ Instructor   ☐ Divemaster   ☐ Buddy

Certification No: ___________

Dive Number: ________________

Date: ________________

Location: ________________

Ocean: ________________

TIME IN	TIME OUT

Bar/psi START	Bar/psi END

SI	PG		PG .

☐ Computer Dive

Bottom Time

Depth

RNT ________
ABT ________
TBT ________

VISIBILITY
____

TEMP: Air ________ Surface ________ Bottom ________

DIVE SHOP STAMP

GEAR USED

BCD: ________________

Wetsuit: ________________

Fins: ________________

Weights: ________________ kg/lbs

Cylinder: ________________ liters

☐ Steel ☐ Aluminum

☐ Fresh ☐ Salt ☐ Shore ☐ Boat ☐ Drift ☐ Night ☐ Training

DIVE COMMENTS

____

____

____

____

____

____

Bottom Time to Date: ________________

Time of this Dive: ________________

Cumulative Dive Time: ________________

Verification Signature

____

☐ Instructor ☐ Divemaster ☐ Buddy

Certification No: ________________

Dive Number: ________________

Date: ________________________

Location: _____________________

Ocean: _______________________

TIME IN	TIME OUT

Bar/psi START	Bar/psi END

SI | PG | PG

☐ Computer Dive

Bottom Time

Depth

RNT ________
ABT ________
TBT ________

VISIBILITY
____

TEMP: Air ______ Surface ______ Bottom ______

GEAR USED

BCD: ________________

Wetsuit: _____________

Fins: _______________

Weights: _____________ kg/lbs

Cylinder: ____________ liters

DIVE SHOP STAMP

☐ Steel ☐ Aluminum

☐ Fresh ☐ Salt ☐ Shore ☐ Boat ☐ Drift ☐ Night ☐ Training

DIVE COMMENTS

____

____

____

____

____

____

Bottom Time to Date: __________

Time of this Dive: ____________

Cumulative Dive Time: __________

Verification Signature

____

☐ Instructor ☐ Divemaster ☐ Buddy

Certification No: _________

Dive Number: _____________________

Date: _____________________

Location: _____________________

Ocean: _____________________

TIME IN	TIME OUT

Bar/psi START	Bar/psi END

| SI | PG | | PG |

☐ Computer Dive

Bottom Time

Depth

RNT ________
ABT ________
TBT ________

VISIBILITY
____

TEMP: Air _______ Surface _______ Bottom _______

GEAR USED

BCD: _____________________

Wetsuit: _____________________

Fins: _____________________

Weights: _____________________ kg/lbs

Cylinder: _____________________ liters

DIVE SHOP STAMP

☐ Steel   ☐ Aluminum

☐ Fresh   ☐ Salt   ☐ Shore   ☐ Boat   ☐ Drift   ☐ Night   ☐ Training

DIVE COMMENTS

____

____

____

____

____

____

Bottom Time to Date: _____________

Time of this Dive: _____________

Cumulative Dive Time: _____________

Verification Signature

____

☐ Instructor   ☐ Divemaster   ☐ Buddy

Certification No: _____________

Dive Number: _______________________

Date: _______________________

Location: _______________________

Ocean: _______________________

TIME IN	TIME OUT

Bar/psi START	Bar/psi END

| SI | PG | | PG |

☐ Computer Dive

Bottom Time

Depth

RNT _______
ABT _______
TBT _______

VISIBILITY
____

TEMP: Air _______ Surface _______ Bottom _______

GEAR USED

BCD: _______________

Wetsuit: _______________

Fins: _______________

Weights: _______________ kg/lbs

Cylinder: _______________ liters

DIVE SHOP STAMP

☐ Steel ☐ Aluminum

☐ Fresh ☐ Salt ☐ Shore ☐ Boat ☐ Drift ☐ Night ☐ Training

DIVE COMMENTS

____

____

____

____

____

____

Bottom Time to Date: _______________

Time of this Dive: _______________

Cumulative Dive Time: _______________

Verification Signature

____

☐ Instructor ☐ Divemaster ☐ Buddy

Certification No: _______________

Dive Number: ___________________
Date: _____________________
Location: ___________________
Ocean: _____________________

TIME IN	TIME OUT

Bar/psi START	Bar/psi END

SI	PG		PG

☐ Computer Dive

Bottom Time

Depth

RNT ________
ABT ________
TBT ________

VISIBILITY
____

TEMP: Air ______ Surface ______ Bottom ______

GEAR USED

BCD: _________________
Wetsuit: ______________
Fins: _________________
Weights: _____________ kg/lbs
Cylinder: _____________ liters

DIVE SHOP STAMP

☐ Steel   ☐ Aluminum

☐ Fresh   ☐ Salt   ☐ Shore   ☐ Boat   ☐ Drift   ☐ Night   ☐ Training

DIVE COMMENTS

____
____
____
____
____
____

Bottom Time to Date: ___________

Time of this Dive: _____________

Cumulative Dive Time: __________

Verification Signature

____

☐ Instructor   ☐ Divemaster   ☐ Buddy

Certification No: _________

Dive Number: ________________

Date: ________________

Location: ________________

Ocean: ________________

TIME IN	TIME OUT

Bar/psi START	Bar/psi END

SI | PG | PG

☐ Computer Dive

Bottom Time

Depth

RNT ________
ABT ________
TBT ________

VISIBILITY

____

TEMP: Air ______ Surface ______ Bottom ______

GEAR USED

BCD: ________________
Wetsuit: ________________
Fins: ________________
Weights: ________________ kg/lbs
Cylinder: ________________ liters

DIVE SHOP STAMP

☐ Steel   ☐ Aluminum

☐ Fresh   ☐ Salt   ☐ Shore   ☐ Boat   ☐ Drift   ☐ Night   ☐ Training

DIVE COMMENTS

____

____

____

____

____

____

Bottom Time to Date: ____________

Time of this Dive: ____________

Cumulative Dive Time: ____________

Verification Signature

____

☐ Instructor   ☐ Divemaster   ☐ Buddy

Certification No: __________

Dive Number: _______________

Date: _______________________

Location: ___________________

Ocean: ______________________

TIME IN	TIME OUT

Bar/psi START	Bar/psi END

SI	PG		PG

☐ Computer Dive

Bottom Time

Depth

RNT _______
ABT _______
TBT _______

VISIBILITY

____

TEMP: Air _______ Surface _______ Bottom _______

GEAR USED

BCD: __________________

Wetsuit: ______________

Fins: _________________

Weights: ______________ kg/lbs

Cylinder: ______________ liters

DIVE SHOP STAMP

☐ Steel   ☐ Aluminum

☐ Fresh   ☐ Salt   ☐ Shore   ☐ Boat   ☐ Drift   ☐ Night   ☐ Training

DIVE COMMENTS

____

____

____

____

____

____

Bottom Time to Date: __________

Time of this Dive: ____________

Cumulative Dive Time: _________

Verification Signature

____

☐ Instructor   ☐ Divemaster   ☐ Buddy

Certification No: __________

Dive Number: _______________

Date: _______________

Location: _______________

Ocean: _______________

TIME IN	TIME OUT

Bar/psi START	Bar/psi END

SI | PG | PG

☐ Computer Dive

Bottom Time

Depth

RNT _______
ABT _______
TBT _______

VISIBILITY
____

TEMP: Air _______ Surface _______ Bottom _______

GEAR USED

BCD: _______________
Wetsuit: _______________
Fins: _______________
Weights: _______________ kg/lbs
Cylinder: _______________ liters

DIVE SHOP STAMP

☐ Steel   ☐ Aluminum

☐ Fresh   ☐ Salt   ☐ Shore   ☐ Boat   ☐ Drift   ☐ Night   ☐ Training

DIVE COMMENTS

____

____

____

____

____

____

Bottom Time to Date: _______________

Time of this Dive: _______________

Cumulative Dive Time: _______________

Verification Signature

____

☐ Instructor   ☐ Divemaster   ☐ Buddy

Certification No: _______________

Dive Number: _________________

Date: _____________________

Location: ________________

Ocean: _________________

TIME IN	TIME OUT

Bar/psi START	Bar/psi END

SI | PG

☐ Computer Dive

Bottom Time

PG

Depth

RNT _______
ABT _______
TBT _______

VISIBILITY
____

TEMP: Air _______ Surface _______ Bottom _______

GEAR USED

BCD: _________________

Wetsuit: _____________

Fins: _______________

Weights: _____________ kg/lbs

Cylinder: _____________ liters

DIVE SHOP STAMP

☐ Steel ☐ Aluminum

☐ Fresh ☐ Salt ☐ Shore ☐ Boat ☐ Drift ☐ Night ☐ Training

DIVE COMMENTS

____

____

____

____

____

____

Bottom Time to Date: ___________

Time of this Dive: _____________

Cumulative Dive Time: ___________

Verification Signature

____

☐ Instructor ☐ Divemaster ☐ Buddy

Certification No: _________

Dive Number: _______________________

Date: ____________________________

Location: _________________________

Ocean: ___________________________

TIME IN	TIME OUT

Bar/psi
START

Bar/psi
END

SI | PG | PG

☐ Computer
Dive

Bottom Time

Depth

RNT _______
ABT _______
TBT _______

VISIBILITY
____

TEMP: Air ______ Surface ______ Bottom _____

GEAR USED

BCD: _________________

Wetsuit: ____________

Fins: _______________

Weights: ____________ kg/lbs

Cylinder: ___________ liters

DIVE SHOP STAMP

☐ Steel   ☐ Aluminum

☐ Fresh   ☐ Salt   ☐ Shore   ☐ Boat   ☐ Drift   ☐ Night   ☐ Training

DIVE COMMENTS

____

____

____

____

____

____

Bottom Time to Date: __________

Time of this Dive: _____________

Cumulative Dive Time: __________

Verification Signature

____

☐ Instructor   ☐ Divemaster   ☐ Buddy

Certification No: _________

Dive Number: ___________________
Date: _______________________
Location: ___________________
Ocean: _______________________

TIME IN	TIME OUT

Bar/psi START	Bar/psi END

SI | PG | PG

☐ Computer Dive

Bottom Time

Depth

RNT _______
ABT _______
TBT _______

VISIBILITY
____

TEMP: Air ______ Surface ______ Bottom ______

GEAR USED

BCD: _________________
Wetsuit: ____________
Fins: ________________
Weights: _____________ kg/lbs
Cylinder: _____________ liters

DIVE SHOP STAMP

☐ Steel   ☐ Aluminum

☐ Fresh   ☐ Salt   ☐ Shore   ☐ Boat   ☐ Drift   ☐ Night   ☐ Training

DIVE COMMENTS

____
____
____
____
____
____

Bottom Time to Date: ___________

Time of this Dive: _____________

Cumulative Dive Time: ___________

Verification Signature

____

☐ Instructor   ☐ Divemaster   ☐ Buddy

Certification No: _________

Dive Number: ___________________
Date: _____________________
Location: ___________________
Ocean: _____________________

TIME IN	TIME OUT

Bar/psi START	Bar/psi END

SI	PG		PG

☐ Computer Dive

Bottom Time

Depth

RNT ________
ABT ________
TBT ________

VISIBILITY
____

TEMP: Air ______   Surface ______   Bottom ______

GEAR USED

BCD: _________________
Wetsuit: _____________
Fins: _______________
Weights: _____________ kg/lbs
Cylinder: _____________ liters

DIVE SHOP STAMP

☐ Steel   ☐ Aluminum

☐ Fresh   ☐ Salt   ☐ Shore   ☐ Boat   ☐ Drift   ☐ Night   ☐ Training

DIVE COMMENTS

____
____
____
____
____
____

Bottom Time to Date: ___________

Time of this Dive: _____________

Cumulative Dive Time: ___________

Verification Signature

____

☐ Instructor   ☐ Divemaster   ☐ Buddy

Certification No: __________

Dive Number: ________________

Date: ________________

Location: ________________

Ocean: ________________

TIME IN	TIME OUT

Bar/psi START	Bar/psi END

SI	PG		PG

☐ Computer Dive

Bottom Time

Depth

RNT ________
ABT ________
TBT ________

VISIBILITY

____

TEMP: Air ________ Surface ________ Bottom ________

GEAR USED

BCD: ________________
Wetsuit: ________________
Fins: ________________
Weights: ________________ kg/lbs
Cylinder: ________________ liters

DIVE SHOP STAMP

☐ Steel   ☐ Aluminum

☐ Fresh   ☐ Salt   ☐ Shore   ☐ Boat   ☐ Drift   ☐ Night   ☐ Training

DIVE COMMENTS

____

____

____

____

____

____

Bottom Time to Date: ________

Time of this Dive: ________

Cumulative Dive Time: ________

Verification Signature

____

☐ Instructor   ☐ Divemaster   ☐ Buddy

Certification No: ________

Dive Number: ___________________
Date: ___________________
Location: ___________________
Ocean: ___________________

TIME IN	TIME OUT

Bar/psi
START

Bar/psi
END

SI	PG		PG

☐ Computer Dive

Bottom Time

Depth

RNT _______
ABT _______
TBT _______

VISIBILITY

____

TEMP: Air _______ Surface _______ Bottom _______

GEAR USED

BCD: ___________________
Wetsuit: ___________________
Fins: ___________________
Weights: ___________________ kg/lbs
Cylinder: ___________________ liters

DIVE SHOP STAMP

☐ Steel   ☐ Aluminum

☐ Fresh   ☐ Salt   ☐ Shore   ☐ Boat   ☐ Drift   ☐ Night   ☐ Training

DIVE COMMENTS

____
____
____
____
____
____

Bottom Time to Date: ___________

Time of this Dive: ___________

Cumulative Dive Time: ___________

Verification Signature

____

☐ Instructor   ☐ Divemaster   ☐ Buddy

Certification No: ___________

Dive Number: ___________________
Date: ___________________
Location: ___________________
Ocean: ___________________

TIME IN	TIME OUT

Bar/psi START	Bar/psi END

SI	PG		PG

☐ Computer Dive

Bottom Time

Depth

RNT ________
ABT ________
TBT ________

VISIBILITY
____

TEMP: Air ______ Surface ______ Bottom ______

DIVE SHOP STAMP

GEAR USED

BCD: ___________________
Wetsuit: _______________
Fins: __________________
Weights: ______________ kg/lbs
Cylinder: _____________ liters

☐ Steel ☐ Aluminum

☐ Fresh ☐ Salt ☐ Shore ☐ Boat ☐ Drift ☐ Night ☐ Training

DIVE COMMENTS

____
____
____
____
____
____

Bottom Time to Date: ___________

Time of this Dive: _______________

Cumulative Dive Time: ___________

Verification Signature

____

☐ Instructor ☐ Divemaster ☐ Buddy

Certification No: __________

Dive Number: ______________________

Date: ______________________

Location: ______________________

Ocean: ______________________

TIME IN	TIME OUT

Bar/psi START	Bar/psi END

SI	PG		PG

☐ Computer Dive

Bottom Time

Depth

RNT ________ ABT ________ TBT ________	VISIBILITY ________________

TEMP: Air ________ Surface ________ Bottom ________

GEAR USED

BCD: ______________________

Wetsuit: ______________________

Fins: ______________________

Weights: ______________ kg/lbs

Cylinder: ______________ liters

DIVE SHOP STAMP

☐ Steel   ☐ Aluminum

☐ Fresh   ☐ Salt   ☐ Shore   ☐ Boat   ☐ Drift   ☐ Night   ☐ Training

DIVE COMMENTS

____

____

____

____

____

____

Bottom Time to Date: ______________

Time of this Dive: ______________

Cumulative Dive Time: ______________

Verification Signature

____

☐ Instructor   ☐ Divemaster   ☐ Buddy

Certification No: __________

Dive Number: ______________________

Date: ______________________

Location: ______________________

Ocean: ______________________

TIME IN	TIME OUT

Bar/psi START	Bar/psi END

SI	PG		PG

☐ Computer Dive

Bottom Time

Depth

RNT ______
ABT ______
TBT ______

VISIBILITY
____

TEMP: Air ______ Surface ______ Bottom ______

DIVE SHOP STAMP

GEAR USED

BCD: ______________________

Wetsuit: ______________________

Fins: ______________________

Weights: ______________________ kg/lbs

Cylinder: ______________________ liters

☐ Steel   ☐ Aluminum

☐ Fresh   ☐ Salt   ☐ Shore   ☐ Boat   ☐ Drift   ☐ Night   ☐ Training

DIVE COMMENTS

____

____

____

____

____

____

Bottom Time to Date: ______________

Time of this Dive: ______________

Cumulative Dive Time: ______________

Verification Signature

____

☐ Instructor   ☐ Divemaster   ☐ Buddy

Certification No: ______________

Dive Number: _________________

Date: _____________________

Location: ___________________

Ocean: ____________________

TIME IN	TIME OUT

Bar/psi START	Bar/psi END

| SI | PG | | PG |

☐ Computer Dive

Bottom Time

Depth

RNT _______
ABT _______
TBT _______

VISIBILITY
____

TEMP: Air _______   Surface _______   Bottom _______

GEAR USED

BCD: _________________

Wetsuit: ______________

Fins: _______________

Weights: ____________ kg/lbs

Cylinder: ____________ liters

DIVE SHOP STAMP

☐ Steel   ☐ Aluminum

☐ Fresh   ☐ Salt   ☐ Shore   ☐ Boat   ☐ Drift   ☐ Night   ☐ Training

DIVE COMMENTS

____

____

____

____

____

____

Bottom Time to Date: ___________

Time of this Dive: _____________

Cumulative Dive Time: ___________

Verification Signature

____

☐ Instructor   ☐ Divemaster   ☐ Buddy

Certification No: _________

Dive Number: _______________
Date: _______________________
Location: ___________________
Ocean: ______________________

TIME IN	TIME OUT

Bar/psi START	Bar/psi END

SI | PG | PG

☐ Computer Dive

Bottom Time

Depth

RNT _______
ABT _______
TBT _______

VISIBILITY
____

TEMP: Air _______ Surface _______ Bottom _______

GEAR USED

BCD: _________________
Wetsuit: _____________
Fins: ________________
Weights: ____________ kg/lbs
Cylinder: ____________ liters

DIVE SHOP STAMP

☐ Steel   ☐ Aluminum

☐ Fresh   ☐ Salt   ☐ Shore   ☐ Boat   ☐ Drift   ☐ Night   ☐ Training

DIVE COMMENTS

____
____
____
____
____
____

Bottom Time to Date: ___________

Time of this Dive: _____________

Cumulative Dive Time: ___________

Verification Signature

____

☐ Instructor   ☐ Divemaster   ☐ Buddy

Certification No: __________

Dive Number: _______________

Date: _______________

Location: _______________

Ocean: _______________

TIME IN	TIME OUT

Bar/psi START	Bar/psi END

SI	PG		PG

☐ Computer Dive

Bottom Time

Depth

RNT _______
ABT _______
TBT _______

VISIBILITY
____

TEMP: Air _______ Surface _______ Bottom _______

GEAR USED

BCD: _______________
Wetsuit: _______________
Fins: _______________
Weights: _______________ kg/lbs
Cylinder: _______________ liters

DIVE SHOP STAMP

☐ Steel ☐ Aluminum

☐ Fresh ☐ Salt ☐ Shore ☐ Boat ☐ Drift ☐ Night ☐ Training

DIVE COMMENTS

____
____
____
____
____
____

Bottom Time to Date: _______________

Time of this Dive: _______________

Cumulative Dive Time: _______________

Verification Signature

____

☐ Instructor ☐ Divemaster ☐ Buddy

Certification No: _______________

Dive Number: _______________

Date: _______________________

Location: ___________________

Ocean: _____________________

TIME IN	TIME OUT

Bar/psi START	Bar/psi END

SI	PG		PG

☐ Computer Dive

Bottom Time

Depth

RNT _______
ABT _______
TBT _______

VISIBILITY
____

TEMP: Air _______   Surface _______   Bottom _______

GEAR USED

BCD: _________________

Wetsuit: _____________

Fins: _______________

Weights: _____________ kg/lbs

Cylinder: _____________ liters

DIVE SHOP STAMP

☐ Steel   ☐ Aluminum

☐ Fresh   ☐ Salt   ☐ Shore   ☐ Boat   ☐ Drift   ☐ Night   ☐ Training

DIVE COMMENTS

____

____

____

____

____

Bottom Time to Date: ___________

Time of this Dive: _____________

Cumulative Dive Time: ___________

Verification Signature

____

☐ Instructor   ☐ Divemaster   ☐ Buddy

Certification No: _________

Dive Number: ___________________
Date: ___________________
Location: ___________________
Ocean: ___________________

TIME IN	TIME OUT

Bar/psi START	Bar/psi END

SI	PG		PG

☐ Computer Dive

Bottom Time

Depth

RNT ______
ABT ______
TBT ______

VISIBILITY
____

TEMP: Air ______ Surface ______ Bottom ______

GEAR USED

BCD: ___________________
Wetsuit: ______________
Fins: _________________
Weights: _____________ kg/lbs
Cylinder: ____________ liters

DIVE SHOP STAMP

☐ Steel   ☐ Aluminum

☐ Fresh   ☐ Salt   ☐ Shore   ☐ Boat   ☐ Drift   ☐ Night   ☐ Training

DIVE COMMENTS

____
____
____
____
____
____

Bottom Time to Date: ___________

Time of this Dive: ______________

Cumulative Dive Time: ___________

Verification Signature

____

☐ Instructor   ☐ Divemaster   ☐ Buddy

Certification No: __________

Dive Number: _________________
Date: _________________
Location: _________________
Ocean: _________________

TIME IN	TIME OUT

Bar/psi START	Bar/psi END

☐ Computer Dive

SI | PG | PG

Bottom Time

Depth

RNT _______
ABT _______
TBT _______

VISIBILITY
____

TEMP: Air ______ Surface ______ Bottom ______

GEAR USED

BCD: _________________
Wetsuit: _________________
Fins: _________________
Weights: _________________ kg/lbs
Cylinder: _________________ liters

DIVE SHOP STAMP

☐ Steel   ☐ Aluminum

☐ Fresh   ☐ Salt   ☐ Shore   ☐ Boat   ☐ Drift   ☐ Night   ☐ Training

DIVE COMMENTS

____

____

____

____

____

____

Bottom Time to Date: _________

Time of this Dive: _____________

Cumulative Dive Time: _________

Verification Signature

____

☐ Instructor   ☐ Divemaster   ☐ Buddy

Certification No: _________

Dive Number: _________________

Date: _________________________

Location: ______________________

Ocean: _________________________

TIME IN	TIME OUT

Bar/psi START	Bar/psi END

SI	PG		PG

☐ Computer Dive

Bottom Time

Depth

RNT _______
ABT _______
TBT _______

VISIBILITY

____

TEMP: Air _______ Surface _______ Bottom _______

GEAR USED

BCD: _________________

Wetsuit: _____________

Fins: ________________

Weights: _____________ kg/lbs

Cylinder: ____________ liters

DIVE SHOP STAMP

☐ Steel   ☐ Aluminum

☐ Fresh   ☐ Salt   ☐ Shore   ☐ Boat   ☐ Drift   ☐ Night   ☐ Training

DIVE COMMENTS

____

____

____

____

____

____

Bottom Time to Date: ___________

Time of this Dive: _____________

Cumulative Dive Time: __________

Verification Signature

____

☐ Instructor   ☐ Divemaster   ☐ Buddy

Certification No: _________

Dive Number: _______________

Date: _______________

Location: _______________

Ocean: _______________

TIME IN	TIME OUT

Bar/psi START	Bar/psi END

SI | PG | | PG

☐ Computer Dive

Bottom Time

Depth

RNT _______
ABT _______
TBT _______

VISIBILITY

____

TEMP: Air _______ Surface _______ Bottom _______

GEAR USED

BCD: _______________
Wetsuit: _______________
Fins: _______________
Weights: _______________ kg/lbs
Cylinder: _______________ liters

DIVE SHOP STAMP

☐ Steel ☐ Aluminum

☐ Fresh ☐ Salt ☐ Shore ☐ Boat ☐ Drift ☐ Night ☐ Training

DIVE COMMENTS

____

____

____

____

____

____

Bottom Time to Date: _______________

Time of this Dive: _______________

Cumulative Dive Time: _______________

Verification Signature

____

☐ Instructor ☐ Divemaster ☐ Buddy

Certification No: _______________

Dive Number: ______________________

Date: ______________________

Location: ______________________

Ocean: ______________________

TIME IN	TIME OUT

Bar/psi START	Bar/psi END

SI | PG | PG

☐ Computer Dive

Bottom Time

Depth

RNT ________
ABT ________
TBT ________

VISIBILITY

____

TEMP: Air ______ Surface ______ Bottom ______

GEAR USED

BCD: __________________

Wetsuit: ______________

Fins: ________________

Weights: ______________ kg/lbs

Cylinder: ______________ liters

DIVE SHOP STAMP

☐ Steel   ☐ Aluminum

☐ Fresh   ☐ Salt   ☐ Shore   ☐ Boat   ☐ Drift   ☐ Night   ☐ Training

DIVE COMMENTS

____

____

____

____

____

____

Bottom Time to Date: ____________

Time of this Dive: ______________

Cumulative Dive Time: ____________

Verification Signature

____

☐ Instructor   ☐ Divemaster   ☐ Buddy

Certification No: __________

Dive Number: _________________

Date: _________________

Location: _________________

Ocean: _________________

TIME IN	TIME OUT

Bar/psi
START

Bar/psi
END

SI | PG | | PG

☐ Computer Dive

Bottom Time

Depth

RNT ______
ABT ______
TBT ______

VISIBILITY
____

TEMP: Air ______ Surface ______ Bottom ______

DIVE SHOP STAMP

GEAR USED

BCD: _________________
Wetsuit: _________________
Fins: _________________
Weights: _________________ kg/lbs
Cylinder: _________________ liters

☐ Steel ☐ Aluminum

☐ Fresh ☐ Salt ☐ Shore ☐ Boat ☐ Drift ☐ Night ☐ Training

DIVE COMMENTS

____

____

____

____

____

____

Bottom Time to Date: _________

Time of this Dive: _________

Cumulative Dive Time: _________

Verification Signature

____

☐ Instructor ☐ Divemaster ☐ Buddy

Certification No: _________

Made in the USA
Monee, IL
07 July 2026